The Civil War Sisterhood

Women Who Made a Difference

by Joan Nichols

PEARSON

Scott
Foresman

Editorial Offices: Glenview, Illinois • Parsippany, New Jersey • New York, New York

Sales Offices: Needham, Massachusetts • Duluth, Georgia • Glenview, Illinois
Coppell, Texas • Ontario, California • Mesa, Arizona

The Abolitionists

Many women who were abolitionists made a difference before the Civil War even began. They wrote books and pamphlets against slavery and spoke out in public lectures.

Sarah and Angelina Grimke were daughters of wealthy South Carolina slave owners, so they grew up surrounded by enslaved people. Yet they were among the first abolitionists. From their earliest years, they believed that all people were created equal.

Hating slavery even as a child, Sarah Grimke said slavery "marred [spoiled] my comfort from the time I can remember myself."

The Grimke sisters moved north to write and speak out against slavery. Many people criticized them, because in those days, women were not supposed to lecture in public. Others, however, were impressed by these former slave owners who spoke out so strongly against slavery.

Because Sojourner Truth was born enslaved, she knew the horrors of slavery from her own life. With a sharp wit, strong voice, and commanding presence, she was in demand as a speaker at anti-slavery meetings.

Angelina Grimke was Sarah's younger sister. In school one day, she was so upset she fainted when she saw an African American boy who had been badly beaten.

Two Harriets

Harriet Beecher Stowe was neither a Southerner nor a former slave. She was a Northerner, born in 1811 in Connecticut, a **free state**. In 1832 she moved to Ohio, another free state, and across the Ohio River from Kentucky, a **slave state**. Here she came in contact with slavery and escaping enslaved people for the first time.

A friend described seeing an African American woman carrying her baby across the icebound Ohio River. Stowe used this story when she wrote *Uncle Tom's Cabin*. Her novel moved her readers and made them see enslaved people as fellow human beings. The novel sold over ten thousand copies in the first week and became a bestseller all over the world.

Supposedly when President Abraham Lincoln met Harriet Beecher Stowe, he said, "So you're the little woman who wrote the book that started this Great War!"

Born enslaved, Harriet Tubman escaped from slavery in 1849. She was so thrilled to reach free territory that she said, "I looked at my hands to see if I were the same person."

While most abolitionists gave speeches and wrote books to fight slavery, Harriet Tubman risked her own life and freedom by helping enslaved people escape. She traveled to the South eighteen times to lead people to the North, where they would be free. Even though there was a large reward offered for her capture, she was never caught.

The Woman Behind the Song

You may have heard the song that begins, "Mine eyes have seen the glory." Julia Ward Howe had heard some Union soldiers singing a popular marching song called "John Brown's Body." The next morning, she wrote new words to the tune and sent them to *The Atlantic Monthly* magazine. Soon "The Battle Hymn of the Republic" was sung all over the North.

The Home Front

After the South **seceded**, the fighting began. On the **home front**, away from the main battles, women fought their own war. Many women worked hard and showed courage defending their homes and supporting the cause in which they believed.

Almost half the men in the North and about 80 percent of the men in the South joined the army or were called up by the **draft**, leaving the family farms and businesses for the women to run. And they did—under difficult circumstances, such as shortages of food and clothing, especially in the South.

Poorer women had to go to work in war industries to support their families. To make ends meet, or just to help the cause, they sewed uniforms and manufactured rifle cartridges.

Despite the additional work, women still found time to help the soldiers. They joined together in their own homes to roll bandages, knit socks, and sew clothing for them. They also sent the soldiers packages of blankets, sheets, towels, and food.

Nurses

More than two thousand women served as volunteer nurses in military hospitals during the Civil War. Most nursed their own husbands, brothers, and other relatives.

For instance, in 1864 Ellon McCormick Looby traveled from New York to Virginia with her four-year-old son John when she learned that her husband Rody had been wounded. She nursed him, and continued working as a nurse in the same hospital until the war ended.

Clara Barton

Clara Barton saw that the Union army was not doing a good job of sending needed supplies to the soldiers or of taking care of the wounded. On her own she sent out a call for food and medical supplies, stored them in her home, and had friends help her distribute them to Virginia and Maryland battlefields. Later, she set up an agency to look for soldiers missing in action and help their families get in touch with them. The experience she gained led to her later founding the American Red Cross.

Sally Louisa Tompkins

Sally Louisa Tompkins opened a hospital in a friend's house in Richmond, Virginia, using money she inherited to run it. The hospital was so successful that she was given the rank of cavalry captain and became known as "Captain Sally."

A Writer and Nurse

Anyone who has read the book *Little Women*, which takes place during the Civil War, will remember that Marmee, the March girls' mother, travels to a military hospital to take care of her wounded husband. Louisa May Alcott, the novel's author, had direct experience of wartime nursing. In 1862 she went to Washington, D.C., to help care for the wounded. She got sick only a month later and had to return home. She wrote about her experiences in a book called *Hospital Sketches*.

Louisa May Alcott

Laundress, Teacher, Nurse

Although born enslaved, Susie King Taylor learned to read and write. When she was fourteen, she was freed by Union troops, even before slavery was abolished. She married Sergeant Edward King of the 33rd United States Colored Troops, a **regiment** of former slaves.

Susie King Taylor

She lived with the regiment—a common thing for women to do in those days—making herself useful by doing laundry and teaching the soldiers how to read and write. When members of the regiment were wounded in a raid, she nursed them. She continued working as a nurse for the next four years.

Woman Doctor in the War

Mary Edwards Walker was one of the few women doctors in the country. The Union army at first refused to let her join as a medical officer, so she volunteered to work without pay, making her the first woman surgeon in the army. Later she did receive an appointment. Captured by the Confederates in 1864, she spent four months in prison. After the war, she was awarded the Congressional Medal of Honor, the country's highest military honor, making her the first woman ever to receive it.

Mary Edwards Walker

Spies

Some women became spies for the Union or the Confederacy. These women learned important military secrets and passed them on to military leaders on their own side. Some acted as **couriers**, carrying messages across enemy lines.

Elizabeth Van Lew

Though a Southerner, Elizabeth Van Lew was a secret abolitionist. She pretended to bring food, medicine, and books to Union prisoners in Richmond, Virginia, simply as a kind gesture. This was the excuse she gave the Confederate guards. Actually, the prisoners gave her information on what they had seen, sometimes in a code she had invented.

Rose O'Neal Greenhow

Rose O'Neal Greenhow had friends among many important people in Washington, D.C., such as politicians and military officers. Using these connections she gathered information and passed it on to the Confederate army. Sent to Europe by the Confederate government as a courier, she drowned on the return journey because her boat capsized and she was dragged down by the gold coins she was carrying to the South.

Elizabeth Van Lew

Rose O'Neal Greenhow

Soldiers

Historians are now discovering that many women—at least four hundred, probably more—disguised themselves as men in order to enlist and fight for the Union or Confederate armies. Some women enlisted to be with their husbands or brothers. Many served out of a sense of patriotism. Others went simply for the adventure and excitement. A few even became spies, and almost all of them fought bravely on the battlefield. Most of these women were found out only when they became ill or wounded. Nurses often discovered these women among their patients.

Canadian Sarah Emma Edmonds served in the Union army as "Franklin Thompson."

Loreta Velazquez wore a false beard and mustache in her disguise as Confederate officer "Lt. Harry T. Buford."

Teachers

As Union soldiers invaded the South, enslaved people flocked to them in search of freedom. Enslaved people who had been freed by the Union army needed food, shelter, work, and medical care. What they wanted was education, because most of them had been forbidden to read and write up until now. Now learning how to do both seemed like the most important thing in the world. Many of the abolitionists and other concerned Northerners who came south to help the former slaves were women who became teachers.

This engraving shows the primary school for freedmen in Vicksburg, Mississippi, in 1866.

Charlotte Forten

Charlotte Forten, a well-educated young African American woman from Philadelphia, had a burning desire to help the freed people. She became the first African American schoolteacher from the North to teach former enslaved people in the South. She kept a diary about her experiences teaching on St. Helena Island, South Carolina.

Glossary

courier a messenger

draft a law that requires men of a certain age to serve in the military, if called

free state a state in which slavery was not permitted

home front the area or activities near home for a country at war

regiment an army group with a large number of soldiers

secede to break away from a group, as the Southern states broke away from the United States

slave state a state in which slavery was permitted